THE BUSINESS PRESENTER'S POCKETBOOK

By John Townsend

Drawings by Phil Hailstone

"Part of every Team Training Manager's presentation kit."
Dr Hubert König, Managing Director, Team Training International, Austria

"This book has helped me, as a working manager, to become an effective and self-confident business presenter."
Graeme Cooper, Course Director, ABIN Bank Training Institute, Germany

CONTENTS

ORGANISING
YOUR PRESENTATION

THE GREAT PRESENTATION SCANDAL

Every year millions of wasted hours are spent giving and attending business presentations. Why wasted? Because most presenters haven't asked why. It's a downright scandal!

And the problem is, they get away with getting it wrong. All over the world it seems that corporate ritual calls blindly for speakers to stand up beside an overhead projector and bore the pants off passive audiences.

Very few of them have the insight (or is it the guts?) to sit down before they start to plan a presentation and ask 'WHY?'.

The result? Millions of hours of useless, droning, self-justifying speeches. Audiences who should be concerned, involved, motivated, simply blocking out the speakers and musing absent-mindedly until coffee or lunch.

ORGANISING YOUR PRESENTATION

THE 3 W's

WHY?

"A wise man asks himself seven times 'why?' before acting."

- Why am I going to give this presentation?
  - To provide information?
  - To represent my function?
  - To entertain?
  - To fill up the agenda?
  - To sell my ideas?
  - To defend a position?
  - To be provocative?

- Whatever the answer, keep asking 'why?' in other ways ...
  - What is the objective I wish to achieve?
  - What is happening **now** that I wish to change or clarify?
  - What will I accept as evidence that my speech has succeeded?
  - What must the audience do or think at the end?

  .....until it becomes obvious **what** your essential messages must be.

ORGANISING YOUR PRESENTATION

THE 3 W's

WHAT?

- Answering the question 'why?' properly will tell you **what** your main messages should be but, however intelligent your audience, they will neither want nor be able to absorb more than:
  - 4 or 5 Keypoints
- Since you have a lot of competition from other speakers (and television!) you need a **vehicle** to carry your message to the audience; after all, if your presentation is not memorable - why bother to speak? Good vehicles include:
  - **A mnemonic device** to link key messages together and help retention (an example is 'Bomber B' on page 6)
  - **An analogy, parable or example** to make a bridge between your messages and the audience's experience
  - **A series of slides** to 'package' your messages

THE 3 W's

WHO?

Once you know exactly **why** you are going to make the presentation and **what** your key
points will be, you must ask, '**Who will be in the audience?**' -
so as to customise your message and make it stick.

- Who are the participants? Level? Background?
- What do they already know about the subject?
- Are they really interested? (If not, I'll have to
  create the interest)
- What are their **WIFM**'s? (**W**hat's **I**n it **F**or **M**e?)
- How fast can they absorb what I'm saying?
- What do they **expect** me to say?
- What is their mind-set (prejudices, attitudes,
  beliefs, etc)?

Tip *To be sure you have tailored your speech to
the audience, play devil's advocate and ask, 'How
could I best offend them if I really wanted to?!'*

ORGANISING YOUR PRESENTATION

STRUCTURE

'BOMBER B'

A mnemonic device to help you structure your presentation and make it fly!

Bang!
- Always start with an attention-getting 'hook'

Opening
- Outline main messages (Route Map)

Message
- Give only 4 - 5 key messages

Bridge
- Make a bridge between each key message and the participant's experience and needs (WIFM's)

Examples
- Give frequent examples to help the audience visualise what you mean

Recap
- Be sure to summarise what you mean

Bang!
- Always finish with a closing 'hook'

Readers of 'The Trainer's Pocketbook' will recognise Bomber B as the nickname of B. Gunar Edeg R.A.F. (B) the Icelandic pilot who helps trainers to structure their courses!

NOTES

Once you've answered the 3 W's and decided on the structure of your presentation, you'll want to start making notes. But, however carefully you prepare yourself, experience has shown that, if you're like most speakers, you'll abandon your voluminous notes as soon as you hit the platform and rely on wordy, boring overhead transparencies or computer slides.

People like Tony Buzan have shown that **KEYWORDS** are all your brain needs to trigger back all the information you've prepared and that **DRAWINGS** and **LOGOS** are even more effective for recall.

You'll find that condensing your notes onto one **A6 CARD** like the example shown overleaf is quite sufficient as a memory aid - and it leaves you free to use bold and simple transparencies, slides and flip charts.

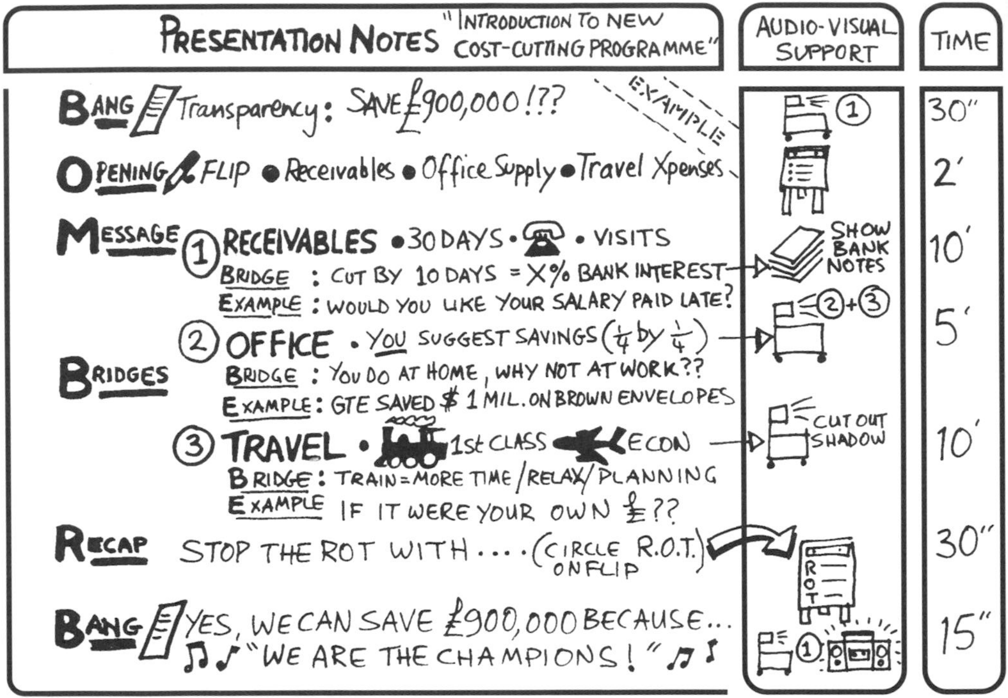
PRESENTATION NOTES
"INTRODUCTION TO NEW COST-CUTTING PROGRAMME"
AUDIO-VISUAL SUPPORT
TIME
BANG Transparency: SAVE £900,000 !??
EXAMPLE
30"
①
OPENING FLIP • Receivables • Office Supply • Travel Xpenses
2'
MESSAGE ① RECEIVABLES • 30 DAYS • • VISITS
BRIDGE : CUT BY 10 DAYS = X% BANK INTEREST
EXAMPLE : WOULD YOU LIKE YOUR SALARY PAID LATE?
SHOW BANK NOTES
10'
② OFFICE • YOU SUGGEST SAVINGS (1/4 by 1/4)
②+③
5'
BRIDGES
BRIDGE : YOU DO AT HOME, WHY NOT AT WORK??
EXAMPLE : GTE SAVED $ 1 MIL. ON BROWN ENVELOPES
③ TRAVEL • 1st CLASS ECON
CUT OUT SHADOW
10'
BRIDGE : TRAIN = MORE TIME / RELAX / PLANNING
EXAMPLE IF IT WERE YOUR OWN £??
RECAP STOP THE ROT WITH .... (CIRCLE R.O.T. ON FLIP)
R O T
30"
BANG YES, WE CAN SAVE £900,000 BECAUSE...
"WE ARE THE CHAMPIONS!"
①
15"

MAKING YOUR PRESENTATION

THE OPENING BANG

Your audience has almost always something better to do with their minds than to listen to you. In order to show respect and make them **want** to hear you out:

Always start with a Bang!

- A provocative or dramatic statement
- A humorous anecdote (not a joke - it's sure to offend **someone** in the audience!)
- Audience participation (a question, a survey of views, a reference to participants, etc)
- An audio-visual 'gimmick' (slide, video, tape, etc)
- An object (a 'prop', a product, a model, etc)
- An action (a demonstration, a mime, an unexpected entry, a song, a quotation, other 'actors', etc)

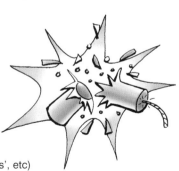

THE FINAL BANG

Most business presentations end with mumbled requests for questions, apologies or other whimpers. Do yourself a favour and:

Always finish with a Bang!

- A statement which dramatically sums up your key message
- A visual or verbal link back to your opening bang
- An unexpected action, happening or apparition
- Simply a determined 'Thank you for your attention' (always 'ask' for applause even if you won't get it)

Imagine ... that each presentation is a gift for the audience. If the 'vehicle' and the structure are the wrapping, the ending bang is the ribbon!

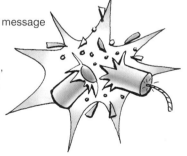

TIMING

Remember the 50% rule.
Rehearse it. Time it. Cut it by 50%. This will ensure that you allow for:

- Late start
- Over-run by previous speaker
- Sharing passing thoughts triggered by the environment
- Participants' questions, etc.

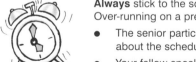

Always stick to the schedule - whatever the consequences.
Over-running on a presentation is **always** bad because:

- The senior participants will conclude that you can't plan and worry about the schedule - and your career!
- Your fellow speakers will resent you taking **their** time
- Non-speaking participants will stop listening and start thinking about coffee or lunch or their holiday in Spain

TIMING

Winston Churchill

(13)

USING YOUR VOICE

PROJECTION — Speak louder than usual; throw your voice to back of room

ARTICULATION — Don't swallow words
Beware of verbal 'tics'

MODULATION — Vary tone and pitch; be dramatic, confidential and/or triumphant

PRONUNCIATION — Watch tonic accents; check difficult words; beware of malapropisms

ENUNCIATION — Over emphasise
Accentuate syllables

REPETITION — Repeat key phrases with different vocal emphasis

SPEED — Use delivery speed to manipulate the audience; **fast** delivery to excite and stimulate; **slow** delivery to emphasise, awe, dramatise and control

NERVES: THE MURPHY MONKEY

As you get up to speak, it's as if a monkey has suddenly jumped onto your shoulders.
He claws your neck and weighs you down - making your knees feel weak and shaky.
As you start to speak, he pulls at your vocal chords and dries up your saliva. He pushes
your eyes to the floor, makes your arms feel 10 metres long and attaches a piece
of elastic to your belt - pulling you back to the table or wall behind you!

Experienced speakers know about the Murphy monkey.
Within the first 30 seconds they throw him to the audience!
When you throw the monkey to one of the participants,
suddenly the spotlight is on them and not on you. How ...?

- A question, a show of hands, a short 'icebreaker'
  (participant introductions, an exercise or quiz, etc)
  a discussion, a 'volunteer' or simply a reference to
  one or more of the participants - all these are ways of
  putting the monkey on **their** backs for a few moments.

  This takes the pressure off you and gives you time to relax,
  smile and get ready to communicate your message loud and clear.

(15)

MAKING YOUR PRESENTATION

DRESS

- Avoid black and white and other strongly contrasting colours

- Wear comfortable, loose-fitting clothes

- If you can't make up your mind, wear something boring - at least your clothes won't detract from the message!

- Try and dress one step above the audience

- Check zips and buttons before standing up

> **Tip for men** *When in doubt, a blue blazer, grey trousers and black shoes with a white shirt and striped tie is usually acceptable from the board room to the art studio.*

LIGHTHOUSE TECHNIQUE

Sweep the audience with your eyes,
staying only 2-3 seconds on
each person - unless in dialogue.

This will give each participant the impression
that you are speaking to him/her personally
and ensure attention, in the same way as
the lighthouse keeps you awake by its
regular sweeping flash of light.
Above all, avoid looking at one
(friendly-looking) member of the
audience or at a fixed (non-threatening)
point on the wall or floor.

BODY LANGUAGE & MANNERISMS

- Don't be tempted by manual props (pens, pointers, spectacles, etc)
- Don't keep loose change in your pocket
- Be aware of your verbal tics and work on eliminating them (ie: 'OK!' - 'You know' - 'and so forth' - 'Now ...')
- Don't smoke (unless seated in discussion mode)
- Watch out for furniture!
- Avoid 'closed' or tense body positions
- Don't worry about pacing, leaning, etc
- Check your hair/tie/trousers/dress before standing up!
- When you forget your body - so will they!

FACILITATING DISCUSSION
SOCRATIC DIRECTION

Take a tip from the Ancient Greeks.

If you wish to encourage audience participation to prove a point use **Socratic Direction.**

K now some of the answers you want
   but know that you don't know everything!

O pen with open questions

P araphrase participants' answers

S ummarise contributions (flip chart?)

A dd your own points

QUESTIONS & INTERRUPTIONS

Most participant questions are not questions. They are requests for the spotlight.
If it's one of those rare, closed **real** questions - answer it succinctly.

If not, first:

● **REFLECT** back to the questioner what you thought was the question:
  ('If I understand correctly, you're asking ...')

Depending on how the questioner 'reformulates' the question, answer it, **OR**:

● **DEFLECT** it as follows:

  Group   : 'How do the rest of the group feel?'
                : 'Has anyone else had a similar problem?'
  Ricochet : (to one participant) 'Bill, you're an expert on this. What do you think?'
  Reverse   : (back to questioner) 'You've obviously done some thinking
                  on this, what's **your** view?'

DEALING WITH DIFFICULT PARTICIPANTS

1. The Heckler

- Probably insecure
- Gets satisfaction from needling
- Aggressive and argumentative

What to do:

- Never get upset
- Find merit, express agreement on **something**, move on
- Wait for a mis-statement of fact and then throw it
  out to the group for correction

DEALING WITH DIFFICULT PARTICIPANTS

2. The Talker/Know All

- An 'eager beaver'/chatterbox
- A show-off
- Well-informed and anxious to show it

What to do:

- Wait till he/she takes a breath, thank, refocus and move on
- Slow him/her down with a tough question
- Jump in and ask for group to comment
- Use as a 'co-presenter' - maybe he/she has some interesting points to add!

DEALING WITH DIFFICULT PARTICIPANTS

3. The Griper

- Feels 'hard done by'
- Probably has a pet 'peeve'
- Will use you as scapegoat

What to do:

- Get him/her to be specific
- Show that the purpose of your presentation is to be positive and constructive
- Use peer pressure

DEALING WITH DIFFICULT PARTICIPANTS

4. **The Whisperers** (There's only one; the other is the 'whisperee'!)

- Don't understand what's going on - clarifying or translating
- Sharing anecdotes triggered by your presentation
- Bored, mischievous or hypercritical (unusual)

What to do:

- Stop talking, wait for them to look up and 'non-verbally' ask for their permission to continue
- Use 'lighthouse' technique

FOOD FOR THOUGHT

- Our Judaeo-Christian work and study ethic have led us to believe that if something is serious, it has to be painful.
  This obviously applies to presentations!

- When we are **participants** at a presentation, we are like pedestrians who criticise road hogs - we complain about boring, long-winded speeches. Then, like drivers who ignore pedestrians, we get up to make **our** presentation and do exactly the same!

MAKING YOUR PRESENTATION

TEN TIPS

- Don't keep your eyes on your notes
- Never read anything except quotations
- If you're not nervous there's something wrong
- Exaggerate body movements and verbal emphasis
- **Perform** (don't act); perform = 'fournir' (to supply) and 'per' (for)
- Pause often - silence is much longer for **you** than for the audience
- Use humour; a laugh is worth a thousand frowns!
- Be enthusiastic; if you're not, why should they be?
- Don't try and win the Nobel prize for technical accuracy
- **KISS** - **K**eep **I**t **S**imple, **S**tupid!

TOOLKIT

AUDIO VISUAL SUPPORT

(27)

VHF COMMUNICATION

The human brain stores information in VHF - as **V**isual, **H**earing or **F**eeling data.

Each participant has a preferred channel for remembering data. In my on-going classroom experiment on recall, 52% of participants say that their memory favours visual information; while only 7% prefer words/lectures and sounds. An astonishing 41% say they remember feelings, tastes, smells and tactile experiences best.

In order to 'tune in' to the maximum number of participants' wavelengths, professional speakers use a wide range of transmitters!

V
- Flip chart • Pinboard • Whiteboard • OHP • Slide Projector
- Props and Accessories • Video clips • Word pictures • Imaging

H
- Music (instant access CD's or Minidiscs for changes of mood/illustrations)
- Sound effects • Audio gimmicks • Onomatopoeia

F
- Music (emotion/mood setting) • Handouts • Verbal descriptions • Anecdotes
- Metaphors • Parables

Feelings stay longer than facts!

PRESENTATION KIT

MASKING TAPE

TIMER

THICK COLOURED MARKERS

PENKNIFE

SPARE ACETATES AND OVERHEAD PENS

FLIP TIPS

PREPARATION

INVISIBLE OUTLINE

CORNER CRIB

READY-MADE

Lightly pencil in headings in advance when unsure of space, drawing, handwriting, etc

Use the top corner to pencil in your notes for each chart. Write small and no one will notice!

Prepare key charts in advance

FLIP TIPS

GRAPHICS

ATTRACTIVE

- Give each flip a title
- Use bullet points (like the ones on this page)
- Use at least 2 dark colours

BIG & BOLD

- Use **thick** markers (bring your own!)
- Should be legible from 10 metres!

CAPITAL KEYWORDS

- Never write sentences!

FLIP TIPS

GRAPHICS

Whenever possible use **cartoons** or **drawings** to personalise and add interest to your headings.

AUDIO VISUAL SUPPORT

FLIP TIPS

GRAPHICS

Standing

Every time you turn your back on the audience your voice and their attention disappear.

Since you can't write **and** face the audience at the same time (unless you are a contortionist!) you should:

- Write (a few words/seconds)
- Turn and Talk
- Write (a few words/seconds)
- Turn and Talk

AUDIO VISUAL SUPPORT

GRAPHICS

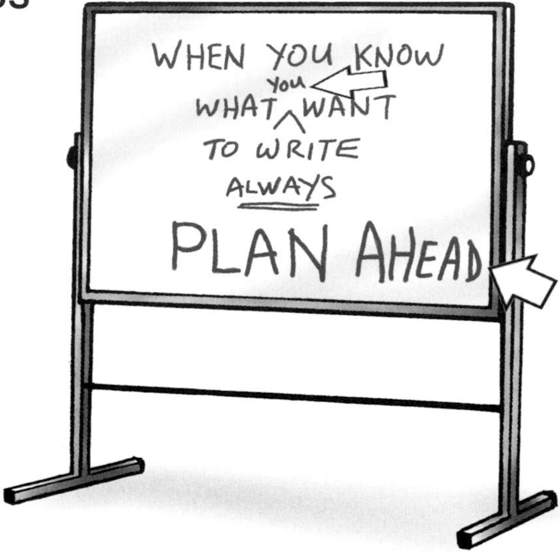

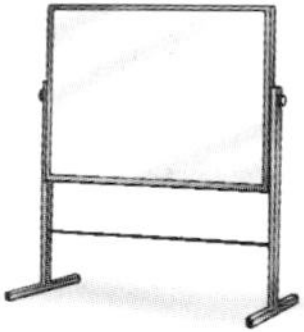

AUDIO VISUAL SUPPORT

O/H & LCD TIPS
PLANNING A PRESENTATION

Use the 'Storyboard' approach

- One transparency/slide with **chapter headings**
- One transparency/slide **per** chapter heading
- One transparency/slide per point/topic in each chapter
- Use consistent design
- Print series name and number on each
- Concentrate message in centre
- Use only $^2/_3$ of space for message

AUDIO VISUAL SUPPORT

O/H & LCD TIPS
GOLDEN RULES

F_{RAME} Use a standard **horizontal** frame with your 'Logo' for all transparencies/slides

L_{ARGE} **Use large, legible letters**
Titles = 1 - 2 cm   Text = 0.5 - 1 cm

I_{MAGES} Use illustrations on all transparencies/slides
Words are not visual aids!

C_{OLOUR} Use 2-3 complementary colours on **all** transparencies/slides

K_{ISS} Keep it simple, stupid!
One idea only per transparency
- Maximum 6 lines of text
- Maximum 6 words per line

O/H & LCD TIPS
PRODUCING TRANSPARENCIES/SLIDES

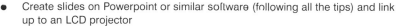

- Create slides on Powerpoint or similar software (following all the tips) and link up to an LCD projector

- Laser print computer-generated visuals directly onto a transparency

- Cut and paste original artwork and text, then photocopy onto a transparency

- Write/draw directly onto a transparency (with permanent or non-permanent pens)

(37)

AUDIO VISUAL SUPPORT

O/H & LCD TIPS
PRODUCING TRANSPARENCIES/SLIDES

Symbols

- Wherever possible use symbols as well as letters

AUDIO VISUAL SUPPORT

O/H & LCD TIPS
PRODUCING TRANSPARENCIES/SLIDES

Freehand Lettering

- Use permanent O/H pens
- Place transparency on squared paper to ensure alignment
- Use colour as much as possible
- Be bold! Practise your own 'alphabet'
- For full letters, use light colour to block in letters before outlining with darker colour

ABCDEFGHIJKLMNOPQRSTUVWXYZ!?

Tip *How about scanning your own titles and importing them onto more classically created computer slides?*

O/H & LCD TIPS

> **Words are not visuals, they are for listening to!**

AUDIO VISUAL SUPPORT

O/H TIPS
USING THE PROJECTOR

PREPARE
- Prepare transparencies in sleeves; in the right order; unclipped

PLACE
- Place a transparency on the projector; align; switch on

POSITION
- Do not block any participant's view of the screen; switch off projector between each transparency

O/H TIPS
PRESENTATION TECHNIQUES

- Use a **Pointer** to highlight messages eg: cut-out arrow, transparent pointing finger, pen or pencil (be careful it doesn't roll off) or a laser pointer

- Place pointer on the transparency and move as you change messages; **don't hold it**; Murphy says your hand will shake!

POINTERS

- Position your pointer here first

- Next move it here

PRESENTATION TECHNIQUES

AUDIO VISUAL SUPPORT

O/H TIPS
PRESENTATION TECHNIQUES

Revelation

- When you have several important
  points on one transparency,
  use a mask to reveal your
  argument step by step
  (if you don't, your audience
  will be reading point 6 when
  you're talking about point 1)

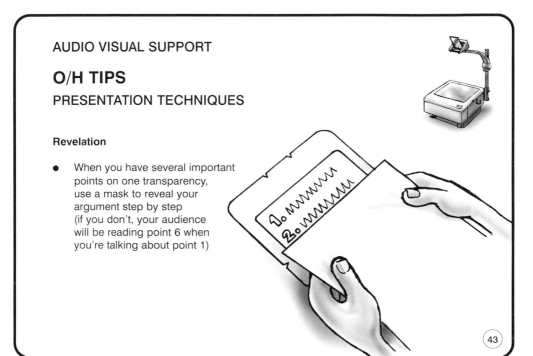

AUDIO VISUAL SUPPORT

O/H TIPS
PRESENTATION TECHNIQUES

Overlay

- Use several superimposed transparencies to build up a story or argument
  NB Make sure you mount your overlays so that they fit onto each other
      exactly - every time

With Plastic Frame (Staedtler)

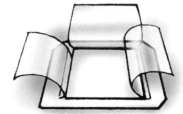

With Card Frame (3M)

AUDIO VISUAL SUPPORT

O/H PROJECTOR RULES
THE PROJECTOR

- Make sure the projector lens and projection surface are clean before
  starting your presentation (if you can't get hold of some glass cleaning liquid and
  a cloth, turn the projector off and use a handkerchief and 'spit and polish')

- Check for a spare projector lamp

- Test projector/screen distance with a sample transparency for positioning
  and focus

O/H PROJECTOR RULES

PROJECTION ANGLE

- How to avoid the 'Keystone' effect

Keep the projector beam at 90° to the screen by tilting the screen (ideal) or by jacking up the projector until keystone disappears; if you jack the projector you'll need a chock to prevent transparencies sliding forward

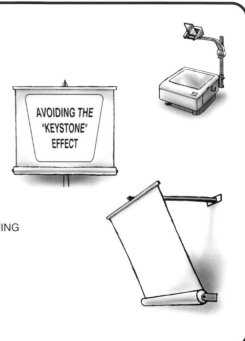

PROJECTOR POSITIONING

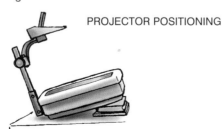

AVOIDING *THE* "KEYSTONE" EFFECT

46

THE LCD PANEL/PROJECTOR

An LCD panel, placed on a powerful (minimum 400 watt) overhead projector, or an LCD projector allows you to display your laptop presentation on the normal classroom projector screen.

- Colourful, professional
- 'Multimedia' animation possible
- Pre-determined sequence of visuals
- No messy acetate storage problems

- Often over-complicated/confusing graphics
- Technically subject to Murphy's Law!
- Easy to forget that words and figures are not visuals!
- Definition of graphics not always as crisp as transparencies

LCD SLIDE RULES

Make sure the person who does your slides will:

- Always use several colours
- Be aware and beware of 'colour camouflage'
  (ie: no yellow on white, blue on green, pink on red, etc)
- Never put more than 6 lines of max. 6 words
  (ideal = what you could write on a T-shirt)
- Use photos, cartoons, drawings as much as possible
- Use a consistent design for series of slides
- Keep words horizontal (especially on pie charts)
- Never show photos of pages from a book
- Remember that words are not visual aids!

PHOTOGRAPHIC SLIDES

WHEN TO USE PHOTOGRAPHIC SLIDES

- When you have the time and the money!
- When you need a 'higher quality' presentation
- When you want to show photographs/cartoons, etc
- When you wish to change pace or differentiate from colleagues' omnipresent overhead slides
- When you wish to dramatise a point and create expectancy by darkening the conference room
- When contact with and participation of the audience are not essential

PHOTOGRAPHIC SLIDES
WHEN NOT TO USE PHOTOGRAPHIC SLIDES

- When you only have words to show
- When you can't darken the room sufficiently
- When audience participation is important
- When you are a persuasive 'eye contact' speaker
- When you have a tight budget!
- When 'everybody else does, so I suppose ...'
- When you don't know how to work the projector

SLIDE PRESENTATION RULES

- Check the projector lamp before going on
- Mark each slide for correct insertion in the carousel
- Do a dry run to check that slides are in the right order and the right way up and round
- Stand away from projector - use remote control
- Use 'black' slides for natural breaks
- Explain what is on the screen - but don't read text
- If you have to talk too - double your enthusiasm and use **PAMPERS!**

THE WHITEBOARD

WRITING & STICKING

Write on!
- Replaces blackboard (school memories)
- Great for brainstorming
- Change colour often
- Only use appropriate whiteboard pens

Stick up!
- Use 3M 'Post-it' stickers to create group-work summaries (key phrases only); stick on whiteboard
- Move stickers into columns or categories; use pens to draw bubbles round salient groupings or to make links between stickers

PINWALL WIZARD

The lightweight, collapsible pinwall is the ideal visual aid for facilitators and project leaders.

Writing   Cover pinwall surface with large sheet of brown paper (from same supplier). Use as flip chart.

Pinning   Distribute coloured cards (same supplier) for exercises/group work. Collect and pin to board in categories. Add headings, illustrations, etc.

Sticking   Cover pinwall with large sheet, spray with contact glue. Stick cards/cut-outs as above.

VIDEO & CD-i

In today's multi-media world, video and CD-i are virtually indispensable tools for professional trainers. Here are some advantages and disadvantages of the medium:

- Professional, fast-moving
- In tune with participants' background/expectations
- Can be adapted to LCD panels/video projection when monitor not available/too cumbersome

- Few videos give **exactly** the message you want
- Expensive to buy/hire
- Technically subject to Murphy's law

 Edit your own video clips at home (2 VCRs needed)
Use only snippets which support your message

AUDIO VISUAL SUPPORT

MUSIC

Here are some ways you should be using recorded music in your presentations:

- To create a friendly atmosphere at the beginning of the presentation as participants come in, meet each other and settle down

- As background music during coffee breaks/intervals

- As an introductory 'bang'

- To create specific atmospheres for special messages (film music, theme tunes, sound effects, etc)

- To illustrate a point amusingly with a song 'snippet' (example for a course on Customer Service: 'Help', 'Keep the customer satisfied', 'You can't always get what you want', etc)

THE CD/MINIDISC PLAYER
VOICE

Recorded speech can be useful for:

- Illustrating messages (Salesman-Customer, Boss-Subordinate)
- Examples of opinions (market research interviews, etc)
- Bringing an absent colleague to the presentation
- Interjecting humorous anecdotes
- Giving examples of current radio ads/trends
- Use a minidisc to record your presentation so you can work on your mistakes

NB When recording audio examples make sure you leave very little space between each recording. In this way you can press the 'pause' button at the end of one example knowing that the next recording is cued to start as soon as you next hit the button.

THE 5 M's

Make Memories, but don't let the Medium Mask the Message!

Ancient Irish proverb invented by Paul Donovan at the Master Trainer Institute.

RELAX!

TOOLKIT

WAIVER CLAUSE

You probably don't have time to spend on creating and using all this colourful and 'gimmicky' presentation support. It's OK! Don't worry, it's optional to be a professional.

MURPHY'S LAW

'If something can go wrong - it will!'

O'Connor's corollary:
'Murphy was an optimist!'

- The only way to beat Murphy is to be a professional and use the 3 P's:

  • **Preparation**   • **Preparation**   • **Preparation**

AUDIO VISUAL SUPPORT

FURTHER READING/VIEWING

'Business Guide to Effective Speaking' by Dunckel and Farnham, Kogan Page, 1985

'How to Master Public Speaking' by Anne Nicholls, Northcote House, 1991

'Painless Public Speaking' by Sharon Bovier, Thorsons, 1986

'Graphics for Presenters' by Lynn Kearney, 5379 Broadway, Oakland, CA 94618, USA

'Memories are Made of This' (video tape), John Townsend, Melrose Films, 1994

'Ten Training Tips' (video tape), John Townsend, Melrose Films, 1994

PRESENTATION CHECKLIST

PRESENTATION CHECKLIST

DISPROVING MURPHY'S LAW

"If something can go wrong - it will!"

Or, as Robert Burns said:

"The best laid schemes o' mice an' men gang aft aglae."

In order to try and disprove Murphy's law next time you have to make a presentation, make sure you:

- Use a presentation checklist
- Go to the conference room the day before the presentation and go through your checklist; make sure you talk to someone responsible about missing items
- Go to the conference room again at least 30 minutes before the start of the morning/afternoon session when you are on and go through everything once again

If it's good enough for Swissair, it's good enough for you!

PRESENTATION CHECKLIST

PRESENTATION	①	②	NOTES
Presentation Notes			
Overhead Transparencies			
Slides/Computer			
Cassettes/Discs/CDs			
Handouts			
Gimmicks			
ACCESSORIES			
Pointer			
Felt Tip Markers			
Overhead Pens			
Masking Tape			
Penknife			
Spare Flip Chart Paper			
Plugs/Extensions			
A/V EQUIPMENT			
Flip Chart			
Whiteboard			
Overhead Projector/LCD			
• Spare Lamp?			
Screen (Tilted)			
Carousel Projector			
• Spare Lamp?			
• Spare Cartridge?			
• Remote Controls?			
Cassette Recorder/Minidisc			
Video Equipment			
Amplifier/Speakers			
Microphone			

TELEVISION INTERVIEWS

TELEVISION INTERVIEWS

MURPHY'S LAW OF VIDEO EDITING

When deciding which extract to choose from your recorded interview, speech or press conference, the editor will always go for the bit which:

- You liked the least

- Shows you saying something controversial (and leaves out any qualification, explanation or proviso you made)

- Supports an argument which the presenter wants to make - regardless of the context in which you spoke

"Did I say that?"

TELEVISION INTERVIEWS

WHAT YOU SAY

The 3 A's

- **Advantages**   Whatever the question or context, stress the advantages of what you're saying/selling for Mr/Ms Everyperson

- **Applications**   Wherever possible turn complicated questions/answers into examples of applications of what you're saying/selling to the lives of Mr/Ms Everyperson

- **Analogies**   Every time you feel that the interviewer is leading you into technical explanations, try and think of simple analogies to illustrate your point

TELEVISION INTERVIEWS

WHAT YOU SAY

The K.I.S.S. Principle

Whenever in doubt **K**eep **I**t **S**imple **S**tupid!

- Very few TV programmes are aimed at people who are experts in your field; even if they tell you that it's for a specialised documentary, the chances are that the 'clip' will be used in a programme with mass audience appeal

SO

- Aim your remarks at the man/woman in the street - without being patronising and without distorting facts

TELEVISION INTERVIEWS

WHAT YOU SAY

Don't knock competition

Avoid making any comments on the weakness of your competitors (unless you're a politician, in which case this is the **only** thing you'll be able to talk about!). Remain non-committal, especially with 'What if ...?' questions.

No names - no pack drill!

WHAT YOU SAY

Avoid making 'Good TV'

Think how TV stations **love** controversy! Any example of live controversy will be sold to TV companies around the world and **always** to your detriment. In fact, interviewers who are hard up for action sometimes attempt to provoke aggressiveness in their questions and behaviour.

Don't be bland, but avoid making 'saleable' television.

TELEVISION INTERVIEWS

HOW YOU SAY IT

Nerves

If you're not nervous, then there's something wrong!

- Breathe deeply and slowly several times before the cameras go live
- Keep some water handy for a dry mouth
- Smile as often as possible; you can't overdo it
- Keep your body language 'open' even when you think you're off camera
  - never cross/fold your arms
  - use open/upward palm gestures
  - keep hands, glasses, pen, etc, away from mouth

HOW TO ANSWER DIFFICULT QUESTIONS

The two-seater helicopter technique

Sometimes an interviewer will surprise
you by prefacing a question with a
value judgement with which you
disagree. ('Some people have
suggested ...' 'It seems to me that ...')

- Smile before you reply

- Get up in a two-seater helicopter and look down at
  the 'problem' as if you were beside the interviewer

- Say something like: 'If you look at it that way,
  I can understand that it seems ... but if you look
  at it another way, then ...'

HOW TO ANSWER DIFFICULT QUESTIONS

Reframing

Interviewers will often 'frame' their questions in a negative way. To reframe successfully you:

- Give a 'receipt' to the interviewer for the question, eg: 'Yes, some people have taken that view recently' or 'I can understand why you see things in this way ...'
- Change the framework or context of the question by continuing: '... but have you ever thought that this means ...' or 'I wonder if people realise that this is because ...'

HOW TO ANSWER DIFFICULT QUESTIONS

One step beyond

With trick questions that try to catch you out on an inconsistency or seeming contradiction in statements, actions or policy:

- Acknowledge the negative bias in the question and then go one step further - towards **your** answer

Example 'Yes, that's true and I'd like to emphasise that this is the very reason for our/my insistence on .... in our/my new programme/action/statement.'

PRESS CONFERENCES

MURPHY'S PRESS RELEASE LAW

However watertight and 'comfortable' your press release sounds to you, at least one of the journalists will take pleasure in needling you on unrelated issues.

O'Connor's Corollary

None of the journalists will stick to the script

JOURNALISTS

Most journalists are terrible questioners in that they are much more concerned with showing you and the other journalists what **they** know than with asking you what **you** think!

GAINING TIME

You will have more time to 'gain time' in a press conference than in a live or recorded TV interview. Whenever you are faced with a question that needs some care, here are some techniques:

● Repeat the question by paraphrasing what you feel to be the key (and most advantageous) element to **you**

● Smile and say, 'Before I answer that specific question I need to explain some of the background ...'

● Deflect the question to a colleague stating why you are deflecting it - thus giving that person an opportunity to gather his/her thoughts

● Take a few moments to discuss the **premise** of the question rather than the answer
Example 'You mentioned that more and more people are worried about...
In fact, a recent survey showed that, on the contrary, people ...'

● Ask the journalist to be more specific with the question

GAINING EMPATHY

1. General

A very general rule that we have discovered about human relationships is that people like people who are not infallible. A major element in interpersonal attraction is the elan of tenderness we feel for open admissions of inadequacy.

Although the press conference is **not** to be seen as an official forum for the sharing of feelings of incompetence, no person should think that s/he has to have **the** answer to every twisted, convoluted question about complex figures, social implications of policy or philosophical considerations of second level abstraction.

GAINING EMPATHY

2. Techniques

- Be relaxed and be yourself
- Smile as often as possible
- Never say 'no comment' but explain **why** it is inappropriate for you to comment
- Don't be afraid to say 'I don't know'
- Avoid sarcasm: don't say 'Unfortunately, Mr Journalist, I have decided to leave my crystal ball in the offices of your esteemed newspaper where I feel it will be used much more often than in our more down-to-earth policy meetings'
- Don't be obsequious or use flattery - journalists are impervious to it
- Never say 'I'm glad you asked that question'; it's the number one no-no with hard-bitten, road-weary journalists

GAINING CONTROL

In order to control a press conference, you must constantly put yourself in the journalists' shoes and ask, If I were representing a newspaper:

- What facts **must** I have in order to construct some kind of story?

- What facts would I **like** to have to make the story more sensational?

- What negative information could help me show the readers both sides of the argument?

- What seemingly unrelated issues/points could I use to colour my main argument (either for or against)?

This mental empathy will lead you to **expect** unpleasant questions and prepare you to counter them with your positive messages.

PRESS CONFERENCES

AND FINALLY!

Remember:

- You can't convince all of the people all of the time

- People only really hear what they want to hear

- You are proud of what you and/or your organisation are doing

GIVING & RECEIVING FEEDBACK

GIVING & RECEIVING FEEDBACK

CONSTRUCTIVE CRITIQUE OF PRESENTATIONS

- Emphasise good points

- Say 'you': address remarks to speaker

- Critique constructively: offer alternatives

Examples

- 'I think it would have been more effective if you had ...'

- 'I'd have been very interested in hearing more about ...'

- 'If we were in a larger room I think people at the back might have difficulty hearing some parts of your presentation'

FEEDBACK CARD

NAME

SPEECH

		NEEDS IMPROVEMENT
WHY?		
• Was the objective of the presentation clear?		
• Had the speaker analysed why s/he was speaking?		
• Did the audience know what to do or think at the end?		
WHO?		
• Did the speaker pitch speech to audience level?		
• Were the audience interested?		
• Did audience resent any remarks?		
WHAT?		
BANG		
OPENING		
MESSAGE		
BRIDGE?		
EXAMPLES?		
RECAP		
BANG		
HOW?		
VOICE		
SPEED		
POSTURE		
EYE CONTACT		
MANNERISMS		
HUMOUR		
GIMMICKS		
VOCABULARY		
TIMING		

AUDIO VISUAL AIDS	FLIP CHART	O/H	LCD	MUSIC	PROPS

MASTERS FOR REPRODUCTION

PRESENTATION NOTES

PRESENTATION CHECKLIST

PRESENTATION	1	2	NOTES
Presentation Notes			
Overhead Transparencies			
Slides/Computer			
Cassettes/Discs/CDs			
Handouts			
Gimmicks			
ACCESSORIES			
Pointer			
Felt Tip Markers			
Overhead Pens			
Masking Tape			
Penknife			
Spare Flip Chart Paper			
Plugs/Extensions			
A/V EQUIPMENT			
Flip Chart			
Whiteboard			
Overhead Projector/LCD			
• Spare _amp?			
Screen (Tilted)			
Carousel Projector			
• Spare Lamp?			
• Spare Cartridge?			
• Remote Controls?			
Cassette Recorder/Minidisc			
Video Equipment			
Amplifier/Speakers			
Microphone			

FEEDBACK CARD

NAME

SPEECH

		✔	NEEDS IMPROVEMENT
WHY?			
• Was the objective of the presentation clear?			
• Had the speaker analysed why s/he was speaking?			
• Did the audience know what to do or think at the end?			
WHO?			
• Did the speaker pitch speech to audience level?			
• Were the audience interested?			
• Did audience resent any remarks?			
WHAT?			
BANG			
OPENING			
MESSAGE			
BRIDGE?			
EXAMPLES?			
RECAP			
BANG			
HOW?			
VOICE			
SPEED			
POSTURE			
EYE CONTACT			
MANNERISMS			
HUMOUR			
GIMMICKS			
VOCABULARY			
TIMING			

AUDIO VISUAL AIDS	FLIP CHART	O/H	LCD	MUSIC	PROPS

THE MANAGEMENT POCKETBOOK SERIES

Pocketbooks

Appraisals
Assertiveness
Balance Sheet
Business Planning
Business Presenter's
Business Writing
Challengers
Coaching
Communicator's
Controlling Absenteeism
Creative Manager's
Cross-cultural Business
Cultural Gaffes
Customer Service
Decision-making
Discipline
E-commerce
E-customer Care
Empowerment
Facilitator's

Handling Complaints
Improving Efficiency
Improving Profitability
Induction
Influencing
Interviewer's
Key Account Manager's
Learner's
Managing Budgets
Managing Cashflow
Managing Change
Managing Your Appraisal
Manager's
Manager's Training
Marketing
Meetings
Mentoring
Motivation
Negotiator's
Networking

People Manager's
Performance Management
Personal Success
Project Management
Problem Behaviour
Quality
Sales Excellence
Salesperson's
Self-managed Development
Starting In Management
Stress
Teamworking
Telephone Skills
Telesales
Thinker's
Time Management
Trainer Standards
Trainer's

Pocketsquares

Leadership: Sharing The Passion
The Great Presentation Scandal
The Great Training Robbery
Hook Your Audience

Pocketfiles

Trainer's Blue Pocketfile of
Ready-to-use Exercises
Trainer's Green Pocketfile of
Ready-to-use Exercises
Trainer's Red Pocketfile of
Ready-to-use Exercises

Audio Cassettes

Tips for Presenters
Tips for Trainers

About the Author

About the Author

John Townsend, BA MA MIPD is Managing Director of the Master Trainer Institute. He founded the Institute after 30 years of experience in international consulting and human resource management positions in the UK, France, the United States and Switzerland.

From 1978-1984 he was European Director of Executive Development with GTE in Geneva with training responsibility for over 800 managers in some 15 countries. Mr Townsend has published a number of management and professional guides and regularly contributes articles to leading management and training journals. In addition to training trainers, he is also a regular speaker at conferences and leadership seminars throughout Europe.

John Townsend, The Master Trainer Institute,
L'Avant Centre, 13 chemin du Levant, Ferney-Voltaire, France
Tel: (33) 450 42 84 16   Fax: (33) 450 40 57 37
E-mail john.townsend@wanadoo.fr

© John Townsend 1985, 1997

Editions: 1st 1985, 5th 1993, 6th 1997 Reprinted: 1998, 2000, 2001.

Published by Management Pocketbooks Ltd, 14 East Street, Alresford, Hants SO24 9EE

Printed in U.K.   ISBN 1 870471 48 2

ORDER FORM

Your details

Name _____

Position _____

Company _____

Address _____

_____

_____

Telephone _____

Facsimile _____

E-mail _____

VAT No. (EC companies) _____

Your Order Ref _____

Please send me:

	No. copies
The Business Presenter's Pocketbook	☐
The _____ Pocketbook	☐
The _____ Pocketbook	☐
The _____ Pocketbook	☐
The _____ Pocketbook	☐

Order by Post

MANAGEMENT POCKETBOOKS LTD
14 EAST STREET ALRESFORD HAMPSHIRE SO24 9EE UK

Order by Phone, Fax or Internet
Telephone: +44 (0)1962 735573
Facsimile: +44 (0)1962 733637
E-mail: sales@pocketbook.co.uk
Web: www.pocketbook.co.uk

Customers in USA should contact:
Stylus Publishing, LLC, 22883 Quicksilver Drive,
Sterling, VA 20166-2012
Telephone: 703 661 1581 or 800 232 0223
Facsimile: 703 661 1501 E-mail: styluspub@aol.com